A Book about Cameras and Taking Pictures

BY GAIL GIBBONS

SCHOLASTIC INC.

New York Toronto London Auckland Sydney
Mexico City New Delhi Hong Kong

TO CYNDI GIORGIS

Special thanks to Andrew Kline of After Image Photography in Montpelier, Vermont, and Bob's Camera Shop in Barre, Vermont

ISBN 0-439-14872-3

Copyright © 1997 by Gail Gibbons.
All rights reserved. Published by Scholastic Inc., 555 Broadway, New York, NY 10012, by arrangement with Little, Brown and Company (Inc.). SCHOLASTIC and associated logos are trademarks and/or registered trademarks of Scholastic Inc.

12 11 10 9 8 7 6 5 4 3 2   9/9 0 1 2 3 4/0

Printed in the U.S.A.   08

First Scholastic printing, September 1999

The illustrations for this book were done in watercolors, colored pencil, and black pen on 140-weight D'Arches watercolor paper.

CAMERA

Taking pictures with a camera can be lots of fun. And the best part is that photographs can bring back memories of family, friends, pets, and special occasions.

PHOTOGRAPH
Also called PHOTO, SNAPSHOT,
or PICTURE

The word *camera* comes from the Latin term *camera obscura*, which means "dark chamber." All cameras are completely closed to light. No light can get inside — except when a picture is being taken.

FILM ADVANCE LEVER

SHUTTER RELEASE BUTTON

BUILT-IN FLASH

FRONT

APERTURE   SHUTTER   LENS

BACK

FRAME COUNTER   VIEWFINDER

12

STRAP

BACK DOOR RELEASE BUTTON

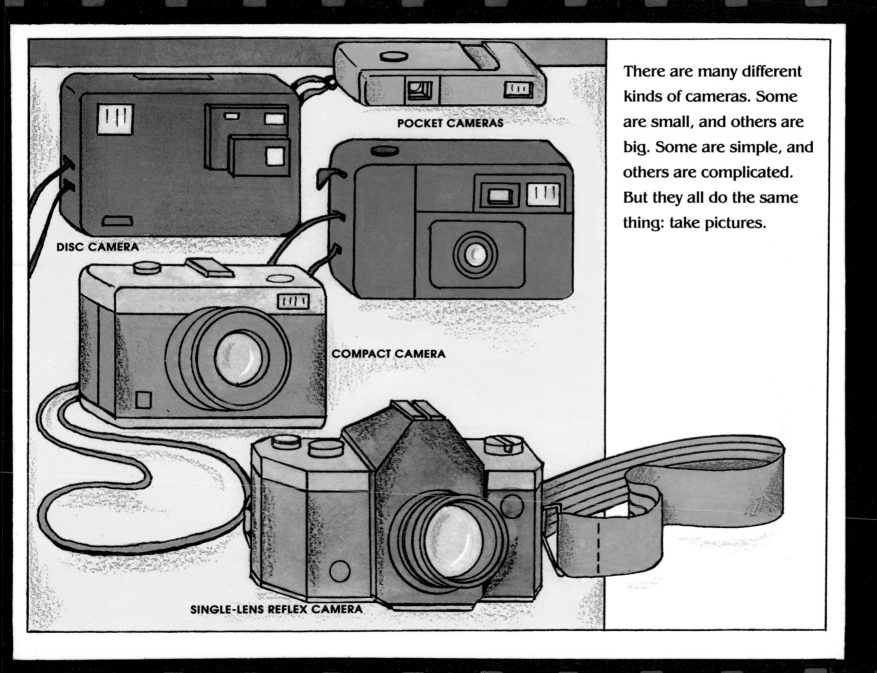

POCKET CAMERAS

DISC CAMERA

COMPACT CAMERA

SINGLE-LENS REFLEX CAMERA

There are many different kinds of cameras. Some are small, and others are big. Some are simple, and others are complicated. But they all do the same thing: take pictures.

It's easy to learn how to take pictures using a simple camera. Here's how to get started.

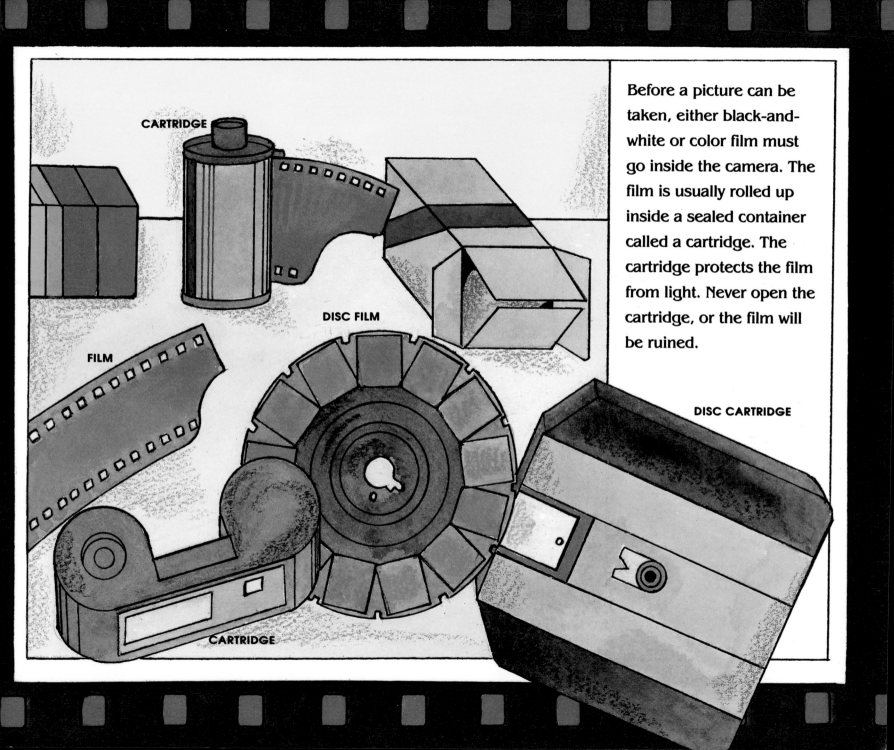

CARTRIDGE

FILM

DISC FILM

CARTRIDGE

DISC CARTRIDGE

Before a picture can be taken, either black-and-white or color film must go inside the camera. The film is usually rolled up inside a sealed container called a cartridge. The cartridge protects the film from light. Never open the cartridge, or the film will be ruined.

Open the back of the camera, and pop in the film cartridge. Some cameras use film that has cutouts along its edges. Place the cutouts over the sprockets to hold the film in place. If you need help, ask an adult. Close the camera.

Some cameras will advance the film automatically. If yours doesn't, turn the film advance lever or wheel until it stops. This turns the sprockets, which move the film forward. The number 1 will show on the frame counter.

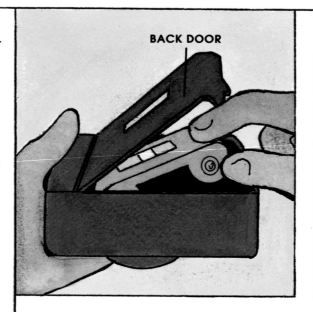

BACK DOOR

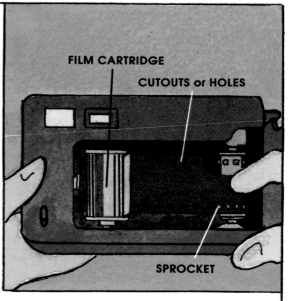

FILM CARTRIDGE

CUTOUTS or HOLES

SPROCKET

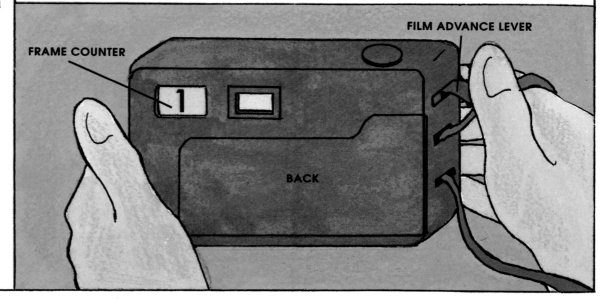

FRAME COUNTER

FILM ADVANCE LEVER

BACK

Try not to wiggle the camera, or the picture will come out blurry.

Make sure your hand or camera strap is not blocking the lens.

Move backward, forward, or sideways until you have framed what you want for a picture.

VIEWFINDER

LENS

It's time to take a picture! Look through the view-finder to see exactly what picture you want to take. This is called framing. The camera has an "eye" called a lens, which sees only what is in front of it.

When everything is framed just right, push the shutter release button. *Click!* Inside the camera, a door called the shutter opens very briefly to let light inside, then closes again. The light passes through an adjustable hole called the aperture. The combination of how *long* the shutter is open and how *much* it opens allows just the right amount of light onto the film inside the camera.

Many cameras set the correct combination of shutter speed and aperture opening automatically.

CLICK!

SHUTTER RELEASE BUTTON

APERTURE

SHUTTER

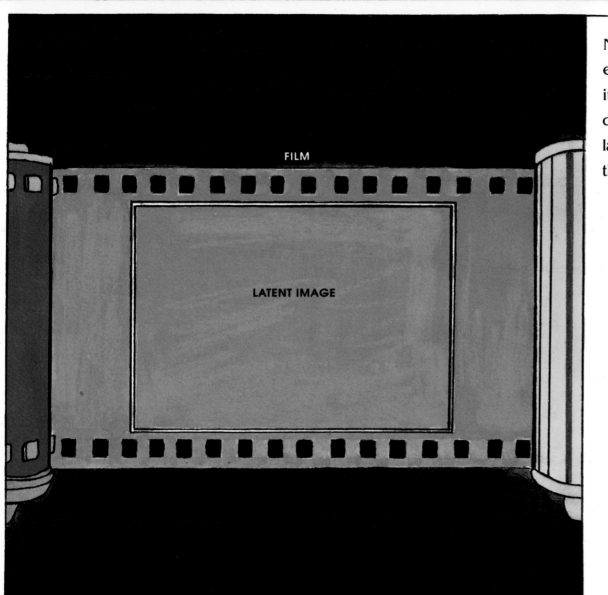

FILM

LATENT IMAGE

Now the film has been exposed. The light has hit it. An invisible upside-down image, called a latent image, is stored there.

The camera has recorded the image shown in the viewfinder when you clicked the shutter. It keeps this image on a special spot of the film called a frame. A roll of film can have twelve, twenty-four, or thirty-six frames. To take another picture, advance the film to the next frame on the roll. The frame counter will read number 2.

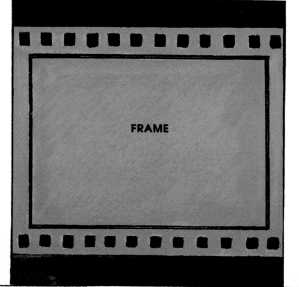

FRAME

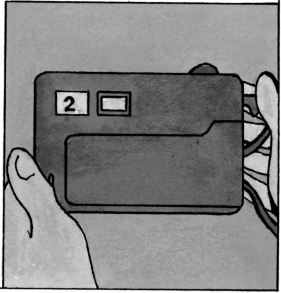

Ready . . . aim . . . *CLICK!*
CLICK! CLICK!

The roll of film is used up when no more numbers appear on the film counter. Your camera may rewind the film automatically. If not, you can rewind it using the rewind button or lever. It's time to take the film cartridge out of the camera and have it developed.

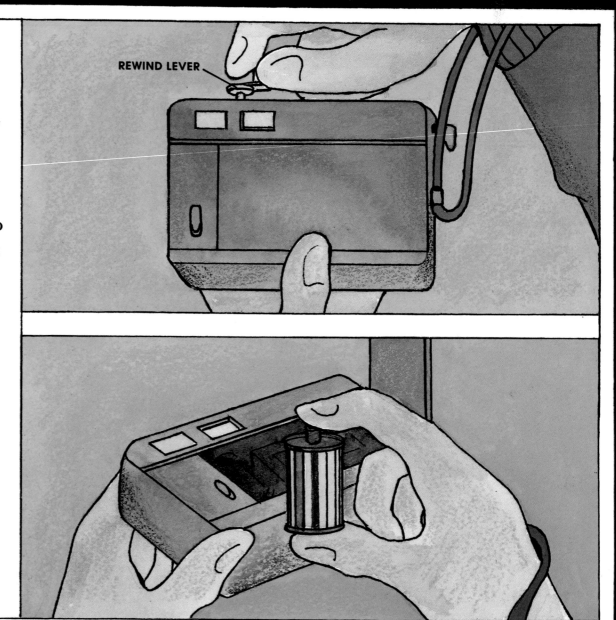

REWIND LEVER

Some photographers develop their own film, but you will probably want to take it to a photo shop. The photo shop will develop the film and print photographs from it. This is called photo processing.

First the film is removed from the cartridge in a darkroom, lit only by a red light. Then the latent images on the film are developed by soaking the film in chemicals. Many places have machines that do this automatically.

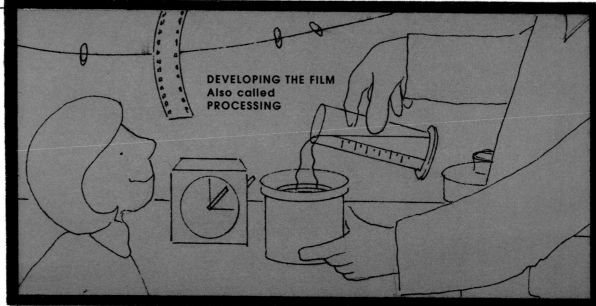

DEVELOPING THE FILM
Also called
PROCESSING

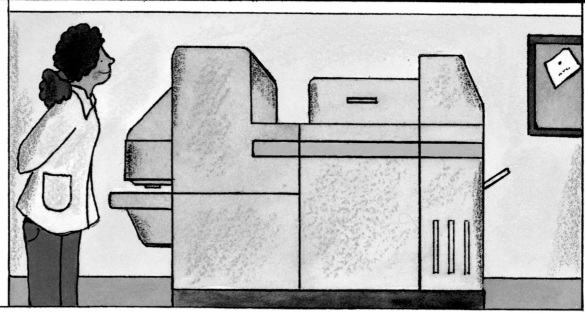

Then light is shined through the film and onto special coated paper. The image from the film is recorded on the paper, although at first you can't see it. The paper is then dipped into chemicals, and the image appears. The last dip of chemicals makes the picture permanent; it is now a finished photograph.

PHOTOGRAPH
Also called PHOTO, SNAPSHOT, or PICTURE

The photo shop returns the photos along with the developed film strips, called negatives. What fun it is to look at the pictures!

NEGATIVES

Always hold a film strip by its edges so you don't leave any fingerprints behind.

STRIP OF FILM

If you hold the strips of film up to the light, you can see tiny pictures. The light areas of each negative are dark areas in each photo.

These negatives can be used again to make copies of pictures. If you want bigger pictures made from the negatives, ask the photo shop to make enlargements.

COPY

ENLARGEMENT

Your camera is fragile and should be handled with care. Never drop it. And don't let go of its strap.

CLICK!

Keep the lens clean with a soft cloth.

Of course, it is important to take care of your camera.

Keep your camera dry.

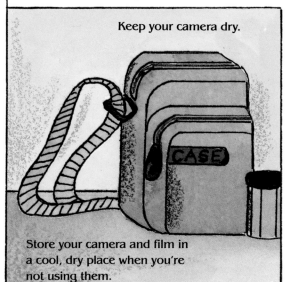

Store your camera and film in a cool, dry place when you're not using them.

Remember, different kinds of cameras use different kinds of film.

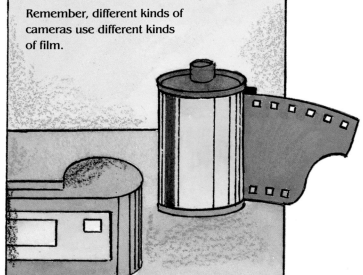

Here are some helpful hints for taking pictures outdoors . . .

Outdoor Pictures

Take pictures only during daylight hours.

Don't take pictures directly into the sunlight. Too much light will get into the camera when the shutter opens. The picture will be overexposed and will look washed out.

Don't take pictures in dark areas or shadows. The picture will be underexposed and will look too dark.

It's best to take pictures with the sun behind or to the side of you.

Indoor Pictures

There is often not enough light indoors for taking good pictures. So most cameras have a flash, which adds extra light when the picture is being taken.

CLICK!

BUILT-IN FLASH

FLASHBULB

CLICK!

FLASH ATTACHMENT

CLICK!

Some cameras use a flash attachment.

If your camera doesn't have a flash, turn on all the lights and make sure the room is as bright as it can be.

Some cameras have a flash switch, which needs to be turned on. You may need to wait for the "flash ready" light to appear before you can go *CLICK!* Some cameras flash automatically when more light is needed.

FLASH SWITCH

. . . and indoors.

"FLASH READY" LIGHT

And here are some helpful hints for taking good pictures anywhere.

Remember . . .

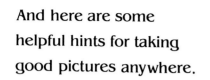

Always ask an adult if you need help when using a camera.

When taking a picture, carefully look through the viewfinder until everything is framed just right. This is called framing or composing a picture. Be patient. Use your imagination!

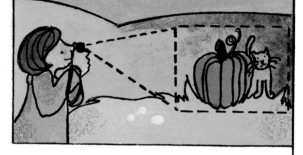

CLICK!

Don't stand too close to what you are photographing. The picture will come out fuzzy. A good rule is to be at least two big steps away when taking a close picture.

You can take many different types of pictures, too.

PORTRAIT

GROUP PICTURE

LANDSCAPE

ACTION PICTURE

STILL LIFE

ANYTHING YOU WANT!

You can make special greeting cards or collages with your photographs, or you can put a small photo in a locket. Pick out your favorite photos, and put them in picture frames. You can even make and decorate your own frames.

It's also fun to keep
pictures in a photo album
to share with others and
remember good times.

The History of Photography

About four hundred years ago, the idea of a camera began in a very simple way — with a darkened room that had a tiny hole in one wall. Light came through the hole, projecting an image onto the opposite wall of the people or objects outside the hole.

In 1826 the first photograph was made by a Frenchman named Nicéphore Niepce [NEE-say-FOR nyeps]. He applied chemicals to a special metal plate, put the plate in a very simple camera, and exposed it to light. From an upstairs window of his house, he took a crude, fuzzy photograph of his barnyard.

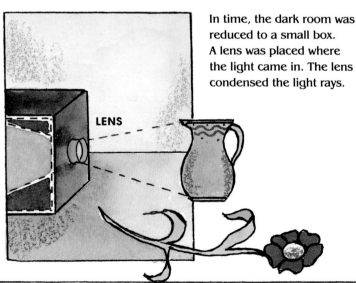

In time, the dark room was reduced to a small box. A lens was placed where the light came in. The lens condensed the light rays.

LENS

DAGUERREOTYPE

In the 1830s, another Frenchman, Jacques Daguerre [zhahk dah-GAIR], was conducting similar experiments. In 1837 he made a clear, detailed photograph of his studio. His system was easier and more practical than Niepce's and soon became popular. These pictures were called daguerreotypes.

CALOTYPE

GLASS PLATE

About the same time, an Englishman named William Henry Fox Talbot invented the paper negative, called a calotype. Paper negatives didn't make very clear pictures. Next, glass plates were used for negatives.

COLOR FILM

In the early 1900s, color photography began. In 1935 the first popular color film was sold. It was called Kodachrome film.

FILM

In the 1880s, an American named George Eastman changed the history of photography. He invented flexible rolled film. He then invented a camera that held a roll of film.

Today cameras come in many different shapes and sizes. Some cameras even develop their own pictures!

Fun Photo Facts

In the 1880s, some people used secret cameras. They were made to look like handbags, hats, books, or even watches.

A picture made from several photos cut up and glued together is called a collage or photo montage.

COLLAGE
Also called
PHOTOMONTAGE

FLASH

The first flash for picture taking was invented in the 1880s. Photographers used magnesium powder, which they ignited with a flint to make a flash of light.

ZOOM LENS

Some cameras have a zoom lens. It can be adjusted to make the subject appear closer than it really is.

Before modern film was invented, photographers had a difficult time taking outdoor pictures. An enormous amount of equipment had to be carried around.

Probably the world's longest photograph was taken in a town in Japan. The 1,284 people who lived there sat on a long row of benches. One hundred cameras were placed every thirteen feet, and all the cameras took pictures at the same time. The photos were made into life-size enlargements and were put together for display.